Essential Lives

CESAR CHAVEZ

CRUSADER FOR LABOR RIGHTS

by Kekla Magoon

Content Consultant:
Dr. Carlos Muñoz Jr., Professor Emeritus
Department of Ethnic Studies, University of California, Berkeley

ABDO
Publishing Company

CREDITS

Published by ABDO Publishing Company, 8000 West 78th Street,
Edina, Minnesota 55439. Copyright © 2011 by Abdo Consulting
Group, Inc. International copyrights reserved in all countries. No
part of this book may be reproduced in any form without written
permission from the publisher. The Essential Library™ is a
trademark and logo of ABDO Publishing Company.

Printed in the United States of America,
North Mankato, Minnesota
052010
092010

 THIS BOOK CONTAINS AT LEAST 10% RECYCLED MATERIALS.

Editor: Mari Kesselring
Copy Editor: Erika Wittekind
Interior Design and Production: Nicole Brecke
Cover Design: Nicole Brecke

Library of Congress Cataloging-in-Publication Data
Magoon, Kekla.
  Cesar Chavez : crusader for labor rights / Kekla Magoon.
    p. cm. — (Essential lives)
  Includes bibliographical references and index.
  ISBN 978-1-61613-512-6
  1. Chavez, Cesar, 1927–1993—Juvenile literature. 2. Labor
leaders—United States—Biography—Juvenile literature. 3.
Mexican Americans—Biography—Juvenile literature. 4. Mexican
American agricultural laborers—History—Juvenile literature. 5.
Agricultural laborers—Labor unions—United States—History—
Juvenile literature. 6. United Farm Workers—History—Juvenile
literature. I. Title.
  HD6509.C48M34 2011
  331.88'13092—dc22
  [B]
                                        2010000565

Essential Lives

CESAR CHAVEZ

TABLE OF CONTENTS

Cesar Chavez

340 Miles

On the morning of March 17, 1966, a determined group of approximately 70 people gathered in Delano, California. The people in the crowd felt a mix of emotions: excitement, nervousness, hope, and pride.

Their leader, Cesar Chavez, had called his supporters together for a special purpose. He had a plan that he believed could change all of them forever. They were all about to set out on the longest, toughest walk of their lives.

Chavez and his friends planned to march from Delano to the state capitol building in Sacramento. It was a journey of approximately 340 miles (550 km). It would take many weeks to walk that far. No one would attempt to walk such a great distance unless they had a very important reason. Chavez did. He hoped the group would run into many people along the way, so that they could tell everyone they met exactly why they were marching.

THE FARMWORKERS' STRIKE

Most of the people in the group were Mexican Americans, who also called themselves Chicanos.

How Far Did They Walk?

Three hundred and forty miles (550 km) is a very long way to walk. It is so long, in fact, that it can be difficult to imagine the distance. It was more than one-third of the length of the entire state of California. The marchers covered about 15 miles (24 km) each day for 25 days. That meant they were walking for about five or six hours straight each day. This was not too difficult at first. But it became very slow and painful later on, as the marchers developed blisters and sores on their feet.

Many worked as laborers on farms and vineyards near Delano. They spent their days picking grapes and other fruits and vegetables on land owned by wealthy farmers. The workers were paid very low wages for long hours of backbreaking work. The farm owners made lots of money selling the produce the workers had picked, but they were stingy about sharing the profits with their employees. Many of the farmworkers were migrants. Migrant workers travel from farm to farm picking different crops.

The farmworkers knew they were not being paid enough, but few other jobs were available to them. Many lacked the education, training, and English-language skills needed to apply for other kinds of work. Often, Chicanos encountered racism when they looked for higher-paying jobs. They worked on the farms because they did not have another option.

The farmworkers quickly became tired of the poor employment conditions. But they did not have much time or money to spend on solving this problem. Many did not believe there was any point in trying. They felt hopeless and trapped.

Chavez did not feel this way, however. He was raised in a migrant-worker family and worked on the farms himself. He knew these struggles firsthand.

*Migrant workers in California labored long hours
under poor conditions during the 1960s.*

In 1962, Chavez had decided to try something new.
He wanted farmworkers to organize a union to
protect their rights as a group. He knew that if all the
workers came together to demand improvements, the
farm owners would have to comply. He established
the National Farm Workers Association (NFWA) and
worked hard to gain farmworkers' support for the

organization. Slowly he gained a following. Workers grew excited about the possibility of better work conditions. But the farm owners refused to respond to the union's demands.

In September 1965, members of the NFWA went on strike. They refused to show up for work until the farm owners agreed to pay them more. They also urged other citizens to boycott, or refuse to buy, grapes that came from the farms whose workers were striking. This would put pressure on the growers.

WHY A MARCH?

Cesar Chavez had already established himself as a leader among the farmworkers.

Migrant Labor

Migrant workers move throughout the year to wherever there are harvestable crops, so they travel a lot. Their lives have very little stability. They may move to a different region each season so that they can catch the peak harvest time for various crops. For example, workers who pick grapes for a while in one area will move on to lettuce until the region has been fully harvested. Then they may travel somewhere else and pick apples or avocados. When the grape season comes around again, they return to where they started.

Some workers travel only a short distance between jobs. They might stay within one state, or region, such as Southern California. Other workers must travel much farther to find work. People who pick oranges in Florida in the winter might travel all the way to Michigan to harvest summer berries, then head to Maine to pick potatoes in the fall. The rotation may change depending on how many other workers are already in each place. It is an inconsistent lifestyle in which the only certain thing is that everything will change again soon.

He believed that the workers needed to stand up for themselves and demand better wages and working conditions. He also knew that the only way farm owners would agree to recognize the union was if their business began to suffer and lose profits without the help of farmworkers.

Cesar Chavez planned the march to make more people aware of the grape boycott and the farmworkers' strike. He believed the demonstration would show the nation exactly how committed these farmworkers were to improving their lives. He thought it could convince more people to boycott grapes. He knew he had to do something dramatic to call attention to *La Causa* (the cause), a movement to which he had dedicated his life.

"When people are involved in something constructive, trying to bring about change, they tend to be less violent than those who are not engaged in rebuilding or in anything creative. Non-violence forces one to be creative; it forces any leader to go to the people and get them involved so that they can come forth with new ideas. I think that once people understand the strength of nonviolence—the force it generates, the love it creates, the response that it brings from the total community—they will not be willing to abandon it easily."[1]

—*Cesar Chavez,
June 1969*

COMMITMENT TO NONVIOLENCE

Cesar Chavez believed strongly that violence was not the answer to the problems his fellow farmworkers were facing. Many workers had become frustrated and angry over their working conditions. Some became impatient with the long-term strike and the slow but steady progress of the movement. They wanted to rise up and attack the farm owners and force them to change their ways. Chavez used his words and his body to convince his friends to resist violence at all cost.

Happy Birthday

Cesar Chavez celebrated his thirty-ninth birthday on the road to Sacramento. It was 15 days into the march. The marchers had reached Modesto, nearly 200 miles (320 km) from Delano. He celebrated with a crowd of hundreds.

Chavez followed the teachings of Gandhi in India and the work of Dr. Martin Luther King Jr. in the ongoing civil rights movement. Like Gandhi and King, Chavez believed that peaceful demonstrations would do more for La Causa than fighting would. The march to Sacramento was just one step in his plan. It was a peaceful way for him to show the world what he and his friends believed and what needed to change.

The March Begins

When Cesar Chavez and the others set out for Sacramento in 1966, they met resistance along the way. Some people did not like what the farmworkers were trying to do. Members of the Delano police department tried to block their way out of town. The police hoped to stop the march before it even began. Still, Chavez did not give up. He talked to the policemen for several hours. He was so patient and so determined that they finally gave up and removed the roadblock so the group could pass.

Though the marchers faced obstacles along the way, they also encountered wonderful surprises. People who had not started out with them joined the march as it passed through their towns. The number of marchers grew. The march started with fewer than one hundred, but soon several hundred had gathered. Shortly after that, the crowd swelled to include a couple thousand people. As the marchers passed through towns and cities, people emerged from their homes to greet them. They presented gifts, food, and drinks, and clapped and cheered for the dedicated walkers. Strangers opened their homes to the marchers, welcoming them for the night. Even those who did not join in the march felt as though they had been part of an important piece of history.

Chavez was thrilled and overwhelmed by the response. Things were going just as he had hoped. Still, the outcome of the march was uncertain. Would the marchers be able to make it the whole

Pilgrimage

In many religions, a pilgrimage is a journey made by a believer to a shrine or to a holy site. People around the world make pilgrimages to places that have deep significance to their faith and culture.

Cesar Chavez and many of the migrant workers with whom he worked were devout Roman Catholics. For them, the march to Sacramento was not only a movement for workers' rights, but also a demonstration of their faith and culture. In the Roman Catholic tradition pilgrimages are an important part of faith. Some Mexicans and Mexican Americans regularly make walking pilgrimages to holy sites within Mexico.

Some of the marchers who went from Delano to Sacramento may have even participated in other religious pilgrimages. Thus, the idea of walking a great distance to reach a goal and to demonstrate a belief was a familiar concept to the marchers.

way? Would the demonstration help people across California learn about the struggles of migrant workers? Would their effort convince the California grape growers to treat their workers more fairly?

The marchers had high hopes, but they did not know the answer to any of these questions. Only one thing was for sure: Cesar Chavez and his friends had a long journey ahead of them. ⌐

Chavez marched with other protesters.

The remains of Cesar's childhood home near Yuma, Arizona

CHILDHOOD

Cesario Estrada Chavez was born on March 31, 1927, near Yuma, Arizona. He was named after his grandfather. His name was later shortened to Cesar when he started school. Cesar's parents, Juana and Librado Chavez, owned a small grocery store, an auto repair shop, and a poolroom. The 160-acre (64.75-ha) farm owned by Cesar's grandparents was nearby. The farm had been in their family since the 1880s. Cesar's early childhood was a happy time. He lived comfortably, though simply, with his parents and five siblings.

THE FIRST MOVE

In the 1930s, Cesar's family began to struggle financially. The economy was bad, and their farm was not making as much money as it used to. The family had never been rich, so losing income was a big problem. Cesar's father had taken out a loan to pay for part of his property. Before long, he could not afford the payments. He was forced to sell the family store.

The Chavezes were not the only family to suffer financially in the 1930s. This was a difficult time for many other people throughout the country. The time became known as the Great Depression, because so many people were out of work and struggling to feed their families or even provide basic necessities.

A Different Spelling

When Chavez's name is spelled in Spanish, it gains two accents. Cesar Chavez becomes César Chávez. The accents are not usually included when his name is used in English writing.

The Chavezes moved in with Cesar's grandmother, Mama Tella. She lived in a small adobe house on the family farm. The farm had cows and horses, as well as cash crops for the family's income. The family enjoyed spending time together.

Mama Tella was nearly 100 years old. She was one of the great influences in Cesar's life. She told him stories and took him to church, teaching him the ways of the Roman Catholic Church. His religious practices would remain important to him throughout his life.

Even though they were very young, Cesar and his siblings did a lot of work to help their family. Cesar worked with his father on the farm. His father often depended on him to help feed the animals and chop wood. Cesar's sister Rita learned how to clean and helped cook for the family when she was only eight years old.

The Great Depression

A depression is a serious economic downturn. The Great Depression began October 29, 1929, when the stock market crashed. People who had invested in the stock market lost lots of money. Some investors lost everything. After the crash, people who had been keeping their money in banks lost faith in the banking system and tried to withdraw their savings. The nation's entire financial system began to fail, as too many people pulled out too much money in a short period of time.

TROUBLED TIMES

While living with Mama Tella, another tragedy struck the Chavez family. The newest addition to the family, Cesar's younger sister, Helena, became very sick. She was only a few years old. The family did not have access to a doctor. Cesar's mother tried everything she could think of to help her daughter get better, but Helena died. It was a sad time for Cesar and his family. Years later, Cesar still remembered that it rained for days when Helena died.

Eventually, the Chavez family lost their farm, as well. They could no longer afford to pay the taxes on the property. On August 29, 1937, the bank came and took away their rights to the land. Cesar was just ten years old. It was a sad and desperate time for his family.

The Chavezes were allowed to remain on the property for a year, even though the bank now owned it. Cesar's father, Librado, went to California looking for work that would allow him to support his family. Finally, the family was forced to pack all of their belongings into their car and head for California. They did not know exactly what they would find when they got there.

Racist Roadblock

Cesar's cousins Ernesto Arias and Frank Quintero took turns driving the Chavez family from Arizona to California. On the first night of the drive, border patrol officers stopped them. Many border patrol officers in the 1930s had racist attitudes. The officers may have been suspicious of the Chavez family because they had brown skin. The family also spoke little English. The officers questioned the Chavezes as they stood on the side of the highway. After five long hours, the border patrol finally let them go.

The Chavez family was lucky. Border patrol officers often

Juana Estrada

As an adult, Cesar Chavez looked back on his upbringing as a big part of why he chose to live his life as he did. He particularly credited his mother, Juana, with instilling in him the beliefs that made him famous. His dedication to nonviolence is an example of the values that she passed on to him.

Chavez's mother often reached out to help others, even when she did not have very much to give. She often sacrificed her own time and money to drive people to the doctor or to the hospital, to feed the hungry, to stand up to unfair bosses, and to support labor strikes.

In his eulogy for her in 1991, Cesar told stories about his mother. He recalled that every night, she would send her children out to invite less fortunate people to eat with them. It did not matter if they only had a very small amount of food for the family. Cesar learned from his mother that sometimes it is necessary to suffer in order to stand up for your beliefs. He would do that often in his life. She also taught him many of the proverbs that he later became famous for repeating.

stopped Mexican and Mexican-looking people and tried to deport them back to Mexico, whether or not it was legal to do so. Through the 1930s, at least 500,000 Mexicans and Mexican Americans were sent out of the United States in this way. Some of them were U.S. citizens.

THE MIGRANT LIFE

Leaving their beloved farm was the first of many moves for the Chavez family. They moved to California's Imperial Valley. Cesar's parents believed they could find good jobs working on farms there. They were wrong. The only work available to them turned out to be low-paying, difficult agricultural labor. They could not earn very much money that way, but they had to take the jobs. The family ended up living in a one-room shack with metal walls and no bathroom or running water.

The Chavez family became migrant workers, moving from place to place as the seasons changed. They took jobs harvesting whatever crops were ready to be picked at the time, such as cotton, grapes, peas, melons, sugar beets, lettuce, onions, and carrots. They planted and weeded, as well, when those tasks were needed. They worked long hours, sometimes

15 hours per day, under awful conditions. They were outside under the hot California sun with no shade and little time to rest. Each time they moved, it was uncertain where they would stay. Sometimes they slept in tents, on the ground, or in their car. For a time, they slept in labor camps with other workers, in huts made from tin and wood.

School Blues

Cesar's mother, Juana, made sure that Cesar and his siblings continued to attend school despite the family's difficult living situations. Juana was illiterate and she wanted her children to have the education that she never had the chance to have.

But school was difficult for Cesar. When he attended schools that were integrated, Cesar often felt like an outsider and faced the racist attitudes of his classmates. Even some of Cesar's teachers felt prejudice against

Big Sister

Cesar was very close to his big sister Rita throughout his life. When they were young, Rita often looked out for Cesar. When he first started school, Rita let him sit by her in class for the first few days. She often helped him with his chores when he forgot to do them.

Rita was very smart and, unlike Cesar, she enjoyed school. Cesar remembered that many teachers admired Rita. Unfortunately, Rita had to quit school after seventh grade to help her family.

Chicanos. Cesar often talked about the challenging experience of going to school:

> *I never liked school. They made me go, so I went, but they always had to push me to go. It wasn't the learning I hated, but the conflicts. The teachers were very mean. I also didn't like sitting in the classroom. I was bored to death. I'd just go to sleep. Once the teacher even sent a note home saying I was ill, that I had to be taken to the doctor because I was always falling asleep.*[1]

The constant moving made school even more difficult for Cesar because he never stayed in one school for very long. Cesar attended more than 30 different elementary schools. He once recalled that he had attended 37 schools in all. He attended some of the schools for a few months at a time. He attended others for a couple of weeks, and sometimes for just a day or two before

Spanish Speaker

The divide between Spanish and English made schooling rough for Cesar. His teachers would scold and mock him if he spoke Spanish in class. Once, a teacher even hung a sign around his neck that read, "I am a clown, I speak Spanish."[2]

Cesar dressed up for his eighth grade graduation. After eighth grade, he dropped out of school.

the family had to move on. He had little time to make friends at school before the family moved again.

Full-time Farmwork

Cesar's childhood was full of anxiety and uncertainty. The migrant lifestyle did not ever allow him to feel safe or secure. He no longer had a sense of home, except what he remembered of life on their family farm. In many ways, that seemed to him like a distant dream. His family was his home now. He had an older sister, Rita, and three younger siblings, Richard, Vickie, and Lenny.

The migrant lifestyle made Cesar grow up very quickly. By the time he was 13 years old he already knew how to drive. Once Cesar and Rita took the car into town without their father's permission so they could get ice cream. Cesar did not have his driver's license yet. He had to sit on pillows so that he was tall enough to see out of the window.

Cesar dropped out of school after he finished eighth grade. He followed in his parents' footsteps, becoming a migrant worker himself. He had done some part-time work with his family before, but now he was out in the heat all day, every day. He was able to bring in a little more money to help their situation. When Cesar, his father, his mother, Rita, and Richard all worked, they would earn approximately $20 per week total. Unfortunately, Cesar also experienced firsthand the poor treatment of workers by the farm owners. He later said of this time, "I went through a lot of hell, and a lot of people did."[3]

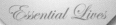

A Glimpse of the Future

The Chavez family settled in the San Joaquin Valley in Southern California. In 1941, when Cesar was 14 years old, members of the Congress of Industrial Organizations (CIO) spoke to his father about organizing a union. This was Cesar's first exposure to the idea of a labor union, or to any kind of organization of workers. This meeting, and the strikes in which his community participated, opened his eyes to the possibilities of workers uniting to demand change. ⌐

Migrant workers in the San Joaquin Valley lived in these small houses.

Chavez worked as a deckhand during World War II.

YOUNG ADULTHOOD

*D*uring his youth, Chavez experienced the difficult conditions that he would spend his life fighting to change. As he grew older, he became tired of migrant work. He longed for something more, something different. But, due to his lack of education and the social biases against his race, he did not have many options. So he kept working.

The United States entered World War II in 1941. Like other Americans, many Mexican-American migrant workers joined the military to serve their country. Chavez was among them.

A SERVICE TO THE COUNTRY

Chavez joined the U.S. Navy in 1944, when he was 17 years old. He went to boot camp in San Diego, California. He felt a duty to serve the country. He also had a desire to get away from farmwork. Chavez did not enjoy his time in the military. But his naval experience did change his perspective on the world. It allowed him to step outside of his familiar, if difficult, world into one that was even more harsh and regimented. Chavez met other people who had difficult lives just as he did. He realized that Chicanos were not the only group discriminated against.

Chavez served in the navy for two years, at the end of World War II. First, he worked as a deckhand on ships in Saipan, located in the South Pacific. One of his jobs was to help ferry ship pilots in and out of the harbors. Later he worked as a painter in Guam. Racial discrimination was a big problem in the military. Chavez was unable to hold any higher post, even a job in the kitchens, because of his skin color.

BACK TO CALIFORNIA

Returning from the service, Chavez went back to California, where he lived with his family in Delano. The city of Delano, like much of the nation, was struggling with significant racial divides. Segregation was still accepted and enforced throughout the area. Often stores would have signs in the windows that read, "No dogs or Mexicans allowed!" Movie theaters were segregated, as well. White people were to sit in one area, while Mexicans had to sit in another.

Chavez experienced racism firsthand. He once defied the movie

A Hero's Return

When Chavez returned to California after leaving the navy, he jumped back into farmwork. His father had remained involved with labor union organizing efforts in the San Joaquin Valley, so Chavez joined him. Within a year, Chavez became part of a cotton pickers strike led by the National Farm Laborers Union. By watching what the leaders were doing, he learned a lot about the benefits and challenges of organizing a strike. He wanted to learn more, so he volunteered to sweep the floors at the union headquarters and did odd jobs around the labor camps so that he could remain close to the action.

Cesar Chavez

theater seating arrangements by sitting in the white section. When he refused to move, the management of the theater had him arrested and taken to jail. He went quietly. It was the first time he was arrested for civil disobedience. It would not be the last.

New Family

Soon after he returned from the war, Chavez began dating Helen Favela. Helen was also a Mexican American from a migrant worker family. They had a lot in common. The couple married on October 22, 1948. They spent their honeymoon touring missions in California.

Eventually, the new couple moved to San Jose, California. They lived in a neighborhood nicknamed *Sal Si Puedes*, which means "get out if you can" in Spanish. It was a poor section of town, mostly populated by Mexican-American migrant workers.

The Chavez Family

Chavez met his wife, Helen, in a soda shop when he was 15 years old. She was one year younger. Also the child of migrant workers, Helen had a lot in common with Chavez. He knew that her upbringing and her values were similar to his own, so he believed she would make a good lifelong partner. Within ten years of their marriage, Helen had given birth to eight children: Fernando, Sylvia, Linda, Eloise, Anna, Paul, Elizabeth, and Anthony. By 2006, the couple had 31 grandchildren.

Seven of Chavez's eight children with their mother,
third from the right, *in 2000*

The families in the neighborhood struggled to
survive with difficult labor conditions, low wages,
and the unkindness of their employers. Many of
them would have liked to move away, but they could
not afford to. Chavez and his new wife were no
exception.

Cesar and Helen Chavez had their first child
in 1949. They would have a total of eight children.
Chavez continued doing migrant labor to support
his family.

They joined a church in San Jose, where the priest, Father Donald McDonnell, inspired Chavez. Father McDonnell encouraged Chavez to read. Chavez read religious texts, history books, and much more. He read about people fighting to protect their civil liberties and about Gandhi's philosophy of nonviolence. Chavez quickly became hooked on reading and went through as many books as he could get his hands on. He discovered that he loved to learn, despite the fact that he had never enjoyed formal schooling.

A Lucky Break

In 1952, Chavez took a job picking apricots in an orchard near San Jose. He met a man named Fred Ross. Ross wanted to meet with Chavez. He kept asking and asking, but Chavez kept turning him down. Chavez was suspicious of Ross. Ross was white, and he came from outside

Chavez's Proverbs

Cesar Chavez became quite famous for using proverbs and sayings in his speeches, letters, and conversations. Some of the phrases he used were:

"The rich have money—and the poor have time."

"We draw our strength from despair."

"We must understand that the highest form of freedom carries with it the greatest measure of discipline."

"God writes in exceedingly crooked lines."

"It's how we use our lives that determines the kind of men we are."[1]

Sal Si Puedes. Chavez did not see any reason to trust him. He feared that Ross wanted to interview him for some kind of study or report on the life of a migrant worker. Chavez had seen things like that go badly in the past, so he did not want any part of it.

It turned out that Chavez was very wrong about Ross's intentions. When Chavez finally agreed to meet with Ross, he planned to sit Ross down and tell him exactly why he refused to cooperate. He gathered a bunch of his migrant worker friends who he thought could help him teach Ross a lesson. Ross showed up to the

---

Community Service Organization

Antonio Rios, Edward R. Roybal, and Fred Ross formed Community Service Organization in 1947. The group's mission was to build a Mexican-American voting bloc and increase political representation for Mexican Americans, in an effort to end prejudice and discrimination. The organization's activities included things such as voter registration drives, political education, and community organizing. It dealt with immigration issues such as helping people become citizens so that they would earn the right to vote. The group worked in some of the poorest neighborhoods in San Jose, including Sal Si Puedes. Later it expanded by forming chapters in dozens of locations across the state of California.

The Community Service Organization made many important changes to the community by registering voters. One of its great success stories occurred in Los Angeles in 1949. Fred Ross and Antonio Rios organized more than 12,000 new Mexican-American voters. The participation of those voters helped elect Edward Roybal to the city council. Roybal was the first Mexican-American member of the Los Angeles City Council since 1881.

meeting, where he faced a crowd of about 20 upset migrant workers. He calmly explained his position. The more Ross talked, the more Chavez changed his mind about ignoring him. Chavez learned that Ross ran a community-organizing group that worked with Mexican Americans and migrant workers to increase their involvement in voting and in politics. The organization also worked to develop labor unions and to fight unfair wages and working conditions. Chavez liked the sound of this group.

Chavez had been working on farms for more than ten years. Almost immediately after the meeting, he started to work with Ross's civil rights group, called Community Service Organization (CSO). Ross was a well-known activist in the area, and he was very good at inspiring, teaching, and organizing people. Ross chose to mentor Chavez because he saw that the young man

Wife's Intuition

Chavez may have been skeptical of Fred Ross's visit. But his wife, Helen, disagreed with his decision to avoid the meeting. Chavez tried to hide from Ross by going across the street to sit in his brother's house until Ross left the neighborhood. Helen took matters into her own hands. She believed that this strange man might present a good opportunity for her family. She pointed across the street to where her husband was hiding. Ross went over to seek him out. Once Ross was face-to-face with Chavez, Chavez reluctantly agreed to meet with him.

had good ideas and great leadership potential. After their first meeting, Ross wrote a note in his diary that read: "I think I've found the guy I'm looking for."[2] This job would help shape young Chavez's entire future. ⌐

*Border patrol officers often checked farmworkers for identification.
Fred Ross helped farmworkers become U.S. citizens.*

Chavez was in his late twenties when he started to work with Fred Ross.

EMERGING LEADER

Chavez's work with the CSO redefined the purpose of his life. The experience helped him understand that Chicanos had the power to change their circumstances. He realized that power was going to waste. It needed to be organized and given direction so that the community as a whole could improve itself.

VOTER REGISTRATION

One of Chavez's first assignments with the CSO was registering voters. The CSO wanted to make sure that Mexican-American voices were being heard in politics. Chavez went from door to door in Mexican-American communities, looking for U.S. citizens who were not yet registered to vote. Once he found them, it was his job to convince them to complete the registration form and come to the polls. Chavez and some friends quickly registered more than 6,000 new voters in San Jose.

The rapid development of this new political bloc gave other political committees cause for concern. Some Republican leaders were afraid these new voters would vote Democrat, so they tried to intimidate first-time voters as they came to the polls on Election Day. Chavez and the CSO protested these practices with a letter to the attorney general. The protest effort backfired slightly.

Voting Rights Act

President Lyndon B. Johnson signed the Voting Rights Act into law in 1965. The law removed all qualifying tests that might discriminate against voters. For example, some districts had previously required voters to take reading tests or otherwise prove they could speak and understand English.

The Red Scare

Chavez did much of his work during a time when Americans were very fearful of communist beliefs. The cold war between the former Soviet Union and the United States was in full swing. The U.S. government had taken steps to ensure that the American economic system of capitalism would not be threatened by the Soviet system of communism.

Capitalism tends to support individual workers achieving success, wealth, and resources through individual efforts. Communism tends to support collective success for groups of workers, and a sharing of wealth and resources among all members of a society. The red scare was a time when Americans were suspicious of communist spies that might be lurking in their neighborhoods. Labor union organizers were believed to have communist leanings, because they wanted more rights for workers, which is one strong theme of communism.

The Federal Bureau of Investigation (FBI) started to investigate Chavez as a possible communist. Even some local newspapers accused him of being a communist. Through this difficult experience, Chavez learned that it was important to stand up to people and to institutions that had power over him. He learned that, through persistence, even one person can win such a struggle.

Expanding the CSO

Throughout the 1950s and early 1960s, Chavez and Ross also worked to expand the CSO by creating chapters of the organization throughout the state of California. Within ten years, they had organized 22 self-sufficient chapters. The CSO was the most effective Latino civil rights group of its time. The strategy of creating local chapters helped with this success. It enabled Chavez

Chavez, far right, worked with the Community Service Organization to promote voter registration.

and Ross to build local leadership and then let those leaders draw in new members and volunteers, rather than having all of the organizing energy centralized in one location at the headquarters.

WORKING WITH FRED ROSS

The partnership between Cesar Chavez and Fred Ross quickly developed into a very effective working relationship. Chavez realized that he could learn a lot from Ross. "My suspicions were erased," Chavez said. "As time went on, Fred became sort of my hero. I saw him organize, and I wanted to learn."[1]

AFL-CIO

Cesar Chavez was not alone in his interest in labor unions. The American Federation of Labor (AFL) was formed in 1886 as a way for existing unions to come together to support each other. In its first 50 years, the AFL had a history of excluding certain groups from its unions. Women, Chinese people, Latinos, African Americans, and other groups were excluded from membership at various times.

In 1935, a group of ten unions broke away from the AFL to form its own federation, which it called the Congress of Industrial Organizations (CIO). The group wanted to protest the AFL's resistance to organizing certain groups of industrial workers. The CIO had fewer restrictions on membership. It included African Americans in its unions during a time when segregation was still common. The AFL and the CIO were both very active rival federations for the next 20 years.

The AFL-CIO was created in 1955 when the two existing labor federations joined and became one again. For a time, the AFL-CIO was not willing to organize migrant workers or allow Mexican Americans to join the organization. Later, it changed that restriction and began working alongside Cesar Chavez to support Chicano migrant workers.

Today, the AFL-CIO consists of 56 national and international unions, representing more than 10.5 million members.

Chavez immersed himself in the work of the CSO. All the while, he observed Ross and tried to learn from him. It worked. Ross recognized a special potential in Chavez. He worked hard to train him as an effective speaker, leader, and organizer. His skills and training brought out the best of Chavez's natural ability to charm and inspire people. Chavez soon began to view Ross as his most important mentor. He never stopped feeling that way. The two men became lifelong friends. They also remained valued colleagues, even after Chavez realized that it was time for him to move on from the CSO.

A NEW CHALLENGE

Between 1952 and 1962, Chavez stayed with the CSO. He became one of its most effective organizers. He learned how to talk to people, how to listen to them, and how to motivate them to act. Chavez rapidly emerged as a leader within the organization and within the Chicano community as a whole. He was promoted to national director of the CSO. He served as an advocate for immigrants and migrant workers. But Chavez slowly realized that he needed to put his skills to a slightly different use.

At the 1962 CSO annual convention, Chavez suggested that the organization work to form

Emma Tenayuca

Emma Tenayuca was born in Texas in 1916. She was a dynamic and creative leader. Tenayuca fought for women's rights and Hispanic rights in a time before either group was taken very seriously as a political force in the United States.

In January 1938, Tenayuca led a strike of 12,000 Mexican women who were working as pecan shellers in San Antonio, Texas. The women went on strike to protest a wage decrease of three cents per hour. The strike lasted several months. Tenayuca was called *La Pasionaria de Texas*, which means "Passion Flower of Texas." This woman's example was an early inspiration for Cesar Chavez, as he began thinking about how to work to improve the lives of migrant workers.

farmworkers' unions. At first the CSO supported the project. Later the group rejected it because the organization was not set up to deal with farmworkers' issues. Chavez decided to take matters into his own hands. He resigned from the CSO. But his work was not over. In fact, it was really only beginning. He turned his attention from mobilizing voters and toward organizing unions and relieving the plight of migrant workers. To do it, he had to return to a world that he had never really left.

Chavez decided to work toward creating a better life for migrant workers.

*Dolores Huerta was one of Chavez's partners
in fighting for farmworkers' rights.*

BACK TO DELANO

esar Chavez resigned from the CSO on
March 31, 1962, his thirty-fifth birthday.
He did not have another job lined up. In fact, he
turned down a good offer from another organizing
group to follow his goal of building a workers'

union. Chavez felt very scared about what might happen to his family if he did not have a job. He talked to his wife, Helen, about how she felt about such an uncertain future. Helen was supportive:

> [We knew] it would be a lot of work and a lot of sacrifice because we wouldn't have an income coming in. But it didn't worry me. It didn't frighten me. I never had any doubts that he would succeed.[1]

Chavez was glad to have his family's support and encouragement. He and his family moved from San Jose back to Delano, a region where there were many vineyards. There were also plenty of Chicano migrant workers, but not a lot of organizing had been started there yet. Chavez intended to change that.

"The greatest tragedy is not to live and die, as we all must. The greatest tragedy is for a person to live and die without knowing the satisfaction of giving life for others."[2]

—Cesar Chavez

NATIONAL FARM WORKERS ASSOCIATION

In Delano, Chavez began putting his organizing skills to use. He held many meetings with farmworkers, talking to them about the power of unions. He wanted them to help him form a union to protect all the workers' rights. Some were easy to convince and eager to get involved. Others were very difficult. They were fearful about the consequences of being involved in such a union.

But Chavez did not give up. He traveled to migrant camps recruiting workers to join the union. He even went into the fields to talk to the workers while they worked. Chavez often worked at recruiting members for 18 hours a day and received little or no pay. Helen took a job in the fields as a fruit picker so that their family could survive without Chavez's income. Slowly, more and more farmworkers agreed to join the union. Chavez's hard work was paying off.

One important leader in the community was Dolores Huerta. Together Chavez and Huerta founded the nation's first migrant worker union. They called it the National Farm Workers Association (NFWA). The first meeting was held on September 30, 1962, in Fresno, California. About 150 delegates attended the meeting. Some even brought their families. They talked about the issues, voted to organize farmworkers, and elected officers for the union. The first order of business would be to lobby for a minimum wage law for farmworkers.

The delegates left full of excitement. Finally, they had united to support La Causa.

La Causa

Chavez worked hard to recruit support for the new union and the cause of migrant workers. He spent the next three years holding meeting after meeting, trying to add members to the NFWA roster. The more people who joined, the more impact the movement would have. Numbers were very important. But Chavez did not just want people to sign up; he wanted them to become involved in the struggle. Sometimes it was difficult to make people understand that they could make a difference. Some felt hopeless, tired, angry, or confused. Slowly, though, Chavez and the rest of the NFWA got the word out and the NFWA membership increased.

Dolores Huerta

Dolores Huerta was one of Cesar Chavez's earliest and most important partners. She is a dedicated organizer who works hard for Latino and minority rights and farmworker rights. She helped Chavez start and manage the United Farm Workers (UFW). She served as vice president of the UFW from 1970 to 1973.

Huerta was brutally attacked outside a hotel in San Francisco, California, in 1988. She was there for the UFW, peacefully protesting Vice President George H. W. Bush's non-support of the table grape boycott. Vice President Bush was attending a campaign dinner inside the hotel at the time. Police began clubbing the protesters. Huerta sustained life-threatening injuries but she survived the attack. The attack was caught on videotape and received public attention. This helped reform police crowd-control methods.

By 1965, the NFWA had recruited more than 1,700 families. However, most farm owners still refused to recognize the union as an organizing body for workers. On those farms, if anything changed, it was for the worse.

Chavez knew it was time for the NFWA to take a strong stand. Up until that point, the union had been fighting the growers with words, ideas, and negotiations. Now, it was time for them to start fighting with their actions.

Labor Leaders

Chavez looked for inspiration from other labor leaders who had gone before him. For example, he studied the work of Eugene Debs and John L. Lewis.

Eugene Debs was a well-known union organizer in the early twentieth century. He was a cofounder of the Industrial Workers of the World, a group with which Chavez would later come into frequent contact. He was also involved in the formation of the nation's first industrial union, the American Railway Union. Debs was a socialist and ran for president of the United States five times on the Socialist Party ticket.

John L. Lewis was a coal miner who became an important leader in the coal mining union in the early twentieth century. He served as president of the United Mine Workers of America for 40 years. Lewis was instrumental in the formation of the Congress of Industrial Organizations. He used strikes effectively to secure wage increases for coal miners, steel workers, and other industrial workers. He worked to improve job safety for these workers and lobbied for laws such as the Federal Mine Safety Act of 1952. Lewis was awarded the Presidential Medal of Freedom by President Lyndon B. Johnson in September 1964.

THE STRIKE

Chavez did not want his union members to use violence to solve their problems with the growers. Some union members wanted to revolt, but Chavez talked them out of it. A strategy of nonviolence was very important to him. He believed nonviolent protests would serve the union better in the long run. He also thought it was the only right way to create change. NFWA members would use large-scale protests and peaceful demonstrations to make their points known.

In the spring of 1965, the NFWA launched its first strike—rose industry workers walked off the job, demanding higher wages. But there was an even bigger strike on the horizon. Later that year, a union of Filipino laborers launched a strike against California grape growers, who refused to recognize the union or raise wages for migrant laborers. At first Chavez did not want the NFWA to join in the Filipino laborers' strike. He was worried his union was

Name Changes and Mergers

The original name of Cesar Chavez's union at the time of the first meeting was simply the Farm Workers Association. It was soon renamed the National Farm Workers Association, to give the group a nationwide focus. In 1966, the National Farm Workers Association merged with another organizing group, the Agricultural Workers Organizing Committee. This was a Filipino workers' organizing group led by Larry Itliong. After the groups merged, the organization was known as the United Farm Workers Organizing Committee.

Filipino workers started a strike against grape growers in 1965.

still too new for something so drastic. But many members of the NFWA disagreed. On September 16, the union put it to a vote and Chavez and the NFWA joined in the strike. The NFWA called the strike *La Huelga*, Spanish for "the strike." Chavez worked hard to promote the strike.

The strike was very difficult for Chavez and the union members. Farm owners and their supporters often threatened and attacked the strikers. Many of them, including Chavez, were sent to jail. However, many people also helped the strikers and supported their cause.

GRAPE BOYCOTT

Chavez knew the farm owners would not cave easily to the union's demands. Many of them were stubborn, greedy, and prejudiced against the Chicano and Filipino laborers. He knew they would not change their practices unless their businesses were somehow in danger. The NFWA added a grape boycott to its strike plan. The group did not want anyone—migrant workers or other citizens—to purchase any grapes from the vineyards that refused to honor the union. They stood outside grocery stores and asked people to join the boycott and not purchase California-grown grapes.

The boycotts began in November and December of 1965. Chavez considered public participation vital to the success of La Causa, but he knew that motivating average people to help would be much harder than it had been to motivate migrant

Building on History

Chavez's idea to create a migrant workers' union was not a new idea. Many people had tried it before. All of them had experienced difficulty creating an effective union.

From about 1900, Mexican Americans had been working to form unions and unite to fight for better work conditions. One of the earliest agricultural unions in California was the Imperial Valley Workers' Union. It used strikes to try to get growers to increase wages and improve work conditions. Another was the Cannery and Agricultural Workers' Industrial Union, which used similar strategies.

When Chavez was young, his father had joined several union attempts throughout Southern California. His entire family participated in a range of migrant worker strikes when he was a teenager. Chavez's background with union attempts was useful when he began to form his own union.

workers. Migrant workers had a vested interest in the movement, but non-workers would not see a benefit for themselves in it. Chavez said, "It is very difficult to get people involved unless what we ask people to do is very simple, very concrete, and very painless."[3]

To get enough people to participate, Chavez knew the NFWA had to make sure that many Americans knew about the grape boycott. He needed a way to draw a lot of media attention to the migrant worker strike and the boycott—and he had an idea for how to do it. ⌐

Chavez, holding sign, and his supporters protested in 1969.

Farmworkers marched to Sacramento in 1966.

MARCH TO SACRAMENTO

havez had high hopes for the planned march to Sacramento. He knew it would be a difficult trip. But he believed the attention the marchers would gain for La Causa and for the grape boycott would make it all worthwhile.

Approximately 70 marchers departed from Delano on March 17, 1966. The group was mostly made up of men. Participants had decided the men should march while most of the women stayed behind to maintain the picket lines and local protest actions. Chavez's marchers consisted of Filipino and Chicano farmworkers. They would walk from Delano to the state capitol building in Sacramento to protest the treatment of migrant workers and to raise awareness of the ongoing grape boycott.

The march succeeded in attracting national attention and support from public personalities and elected officials. The marchers received responses from both extremes—some people tried to attack them along the way, but other people fed, cheered, and supported them as they passed. At several points during the march, other farmworkers simply walked off the job and joined the strike and the march.

The walking took a physical toll on Chavez. He had been so busy setting up the march that he had not taken time in the days before he left

Flags Flying High

During the march to Sacramento, workers carried four flags at the front of the procession: the American flag, the Mexican flag, the flag of the Philippines, and the banner of Our Lady of Guadalupe. Others in the crowd carried flags and wore armbands with a red background and a black eagle, the logo of the NFWA.

to get himself a good pair of walking shoes. Within the first week, he had terrible blisters on his feet.

His legs swelled, first at the ankle, then all the way up to his knees. On the seventh day, it became impossible for him to walk. He had a high fever and was very ill. But the march had to continue. The other walkers put Chavez in the back of a car, and he had to ride alongside them for a few days. By the end of the second week, his legs had healed, and he rejoined the march under his own power.

The Plan of Delano

The NFWA outlined its goals for farm-worker rights in *El Plan de Delano* (The Plan of Delano):

We the undersigned, gathered in Pilgrimage to the capital of the State in Sacramento in penance for all the failings of Farm Workers, as free and sovereign men, do solemnly declare before the civilized world which judges our actions, and before the nation to which we belong, the propositions we have formulated to end the injustice that oppresses us.

1. This is the beginning of a social movement in fact and not in pronouncements. We seek our basic, God-given rights as human beings.

2. We seek the support of all political groups and protection of the government, which is also our government, in our struggle.

3. We seek, and have, the support of the Church in what we do. At the head of the Pilgrimage we carry La Virgen de la Guadalupe (The Virgin of Guadalupe) because she is ours, all ours, Patroness of the Mexican people.

4. We are suffering.

5. We shall unite.

6. We will strike.[1]

A Glimpse of Success

Seventeen days into the march, Chavez received a call from a representative of one of the grape growers, the Schenley Corporation, requesting a meeting with him. At first he would not take the call. He was nervous, fearing the corporation would lead him into a trap. But he went to the meeting anyway, because he had to know for sure what the Schenley Corporation wanted.

It was fortunate that Chavez chose to meet with the Schenley Corporation. Schenley had decided to respect the union's request. It was prepared to negotiate an increase in wages for its farmworkers. The strike had begun to work. Chavez negotiated the deal, and then he returned to his friends. They had to finish the march. The farmworkers still had many miles to go before reaching Sacramento. Even though one grape grower had changed, it was

The Bracero Program

One complication to the early strike plans was the Bracero Program. Braceros were immigrant laborers. The Bracero Program, which began in 1942 to alleviate labor shortages during World War II, allowed farm owners to bring braceros out of Mexico to harvest crops. After the war, farm owners used braceros to replace the striking farmworkers. Under the law, braceros could only be used to make up for a documented labor shortage. But farm owners ignored this rule often.

The Mexican-American migrant workers protested the use of imported labor. They argued that it was not fair for farm owners to be able to bring in workers when the unions were striking, as that defeated the purpose of union organizing. The Bracero Program made it difficult for worker strikes to be taken seriously.

Chavez waved to the crowd from the capitol steps on April 10, 1966.

not enough to stop the movement. La Causa and the march continued.

SACRAMENTO

The marchers arrived in Sacramento on April 10, 1966, in a crowd that had grown to more than 10,000 people. It was Easter Sunday, which made it a particularly special moment for Catholics and other Christians among the marchers. Chavez climbed the steps of the capitol building and made a speech in which he celebrated the success of their journey and praised all who had participated. The crowd gave an honored place to the more than 60 marchers who had made it all the way from Delano. The march had lasted 25 days from beginning to end.

When Chavez announced the successful negotiation with Schenley, the crowd became jubilant. They feasted and celebrated what they hoped would be the first of many similar victories. They were proud of what they had accomplished.

Following the success of the march, the Chicano and Filipino workers decided to merge their unions into one. The new union name would be United Farm Workers' Organizing Committee. The organization would eventually be called United Farm Workers of America (UFW).

The march to Sacramento gave good publicity to the grape boycott. But it did not do much to actually persuade the grape growers to change their policies. Chavez and his followers still had work ahead of them. The strike would continue.

"Our boycotts are predicated on faith in the basic compassion of people everywhere. We are convinced that when consumers are faced with a direct appeal from the poor struggling against great odds, they will react positively. The American people still yearn for justice."[2]

—*Cesar Chavez*

CHAVEZ SPEAKS UP AGAINST DIGIORGIO

Chavez's meetings with the growers did not always go well. Just three days after the march ended in Sacramento, union members started a strike and boycott of another grower, DiGiorgio Fruit Corp. Because of his leadership position, Chavez met with DiGiorgio representatives to negotiate. However, while he was in talks with a vice president of the company, Chavez received a disturbing phone call. On the phone was someone from the union. Chavez learned that some DiGiorgio guards and employees had attacked picketers and the picketers had been sent to jail.

Chavez was furious. He was trying to lead a nonviolent movement. Chavez went back into the room and told the DiGiorgio representatives that he would not negotiate with them if they allowed their employees

Following in Gandhi's Footsteps

Cesar Chavez arrived at many of his ideas, beliefs, and actions by studying the teachings of Mohandas K. Gandhi. Gandhi was a political and spiritual leader of the Indian independence movement. He was called "Mahatma" by his followers, a Sanskrit word that means "great soul."

Gandhi mobilized millions to stand up in nonviolent demonstrations to protest British colonial rule in India. Great Britain finally released India from its control after World War II.

Just as the independent India was building itself, Gandhi was shot to death in New Delhi, India, on January 30, 1948. Gandhi's influence is still felt. His principles were used in the U.S. civil rights movement, the anti-apartheid movement in South Africa, and Cesar Chavez's workers' rights movement.

to hurt the picketers. Chavez must have made an impression because the company took the guns away from their guards.

LEANING TOWARD VIOLENCE

Although Chavez had led a successful march and attracted national attention, more difficulties lay ahead. Many union members gradually became frustrated with the ongoing strike. Nothing was changing, they argued. They found the lack of progress discouraging. They felt that the movement was not accomplishing anything anymore. Chavez tried to reason with them. He believed that progress was happening, just very slowly. Chavez was set on following the teachings of Gandhi, whom he had admired for many years. Chavez thought that patience and perseverance would make their efforts succeed in the long run. But as time went on, it became harder for him to convince the union members to stick with a nonviolent approach.

A series of attacks on farmworkers by the grape growers agitated the union members. Some began to respond to the grape growers' violent acts with violence of their own. Chavez discovered that people had started bringing guns to the picket lines, just in case they needed the firearms. He became very distressed by these actions. He needed to get through to the union members somehow and to convince them to follow him. He had to come up with a plan to get their attention and persuade them that nonviolent protest was the only way for the union to achieve its goals. Chavez explained what he did next:

> I thought that I had to bring the Movement to a halt, do something that would force them and me to deal with the whole question of violence and ourselves. We had to stop long enough to take account of what we were doing. So I stopped eating.[3]

Chavez had much support from other farmworkers, but some disagreed with his insistence on nonviolent protest.

Chavez became very thin when he fasted.

FASTING, STRIKES, AND BOYCOTTS

Chavez believed that the ongoing labor strikes, boycotts, and acts of civil disobedience were working. These efforts had begun to raise consciousness of the plight of Mexican-American farmworkers. But when his union colleagues began turning to violence, once again Chavez needed to do something drastic to get his point across.

On February 16, 1968, Cesar Chavez began fasting. He stopped eating all food. He stopped drinking all beverages except water. At first the fast was a secret. Chavez did not tell anyone what he was doing. He did not know how long he was going to keep the fast.

The first few days were quite rough on him. He had stomach pains, body aches, and dreams and nightmares about food. One of his colleagues, LeRoy Chatfield, learned what Chavez was doing and began helping him. Chatfield drove him to and from work, and gave him calorie-free soda to drink.

After four days of private fasting, Chavez made a decision. He called a meeting with his staff and all the union strikers. They met at Filipino Hall, where Chavez made a short speech about his commitment to nonviolence. He announced to his followers that he would not eat again until everyone involved in the strike either completely ignored him or committed to practicing nonviolence. He then walked out of the hall. The union members were shocked.

Helen Chavez's Concerns

When Chavez walked out of Filipino Hall after making his speech, his wife, Helen, followed after him. They argued about his decision to fast. She told

him she thought it was ridiculous. She accused him of making a reckless decision, and not thinking about his family. But she knew he would not change his mind.

At the time, Chavez was upset because he thought his wife was not being supportive of him. Later, he understood why she had reacted so strongly. Helen was worried that Chavez would die as a result of the fast.

Fasting

A fast is a deliberate decision a person makes to limit his or her food intake for a short period of time. The human body can only survive for a few days without water. Without food, the body may be able to last several weeks, but it quickly begins to weaken.

People undertake fasts for a variety of reasons. Many do it for religious fulfillment. Religious traditions, such as Buddhism, Hinduism, and Christianity, incorporate fasting into their beliefs. Others do it for medical reasons, such as preparing for a surgical procedure. Those kinds of fasts usually remain private. Public fasting is usually done as a means to protest an injustice or to support something the faster believes in. This was the way Chavez used his fasts.

Fasting does not necessarily mean a person has stopped eating altogether. It may mean eliminating a certain food, such as meat or bread, from one's diet. For example, during Passover, Jewish people do not eat bread made with yeast. A fast may also mean refraining from all food during a certain part of the day. During Ramadan, Muslims do not eat during daylight hours, but they feast after sundown.

FORTY ACRES

Chavez decided not to fast at home. He moved out to Forty Acres, a plot of land near Delano that had become the UFW headquarters. At Forty Acres, he could rest but still hold meetings with people. The community responded to his fast. People immediately began denouncing violence and flocked to Forty Acres to help care for Chavez.

Not very many people supported Chavez in his decision to fast. People came to talk him out of it, or to pray for him, or because they were worried that he was putting his life at risk. But Chavez saw that his fast had motivated people to work harder for La Causa, and it had generated good press and new political energy for the movement. So he kept fasting.

After about a week, Chavez found he was no longer having hunger pains. He did not crave food in the way he had in the first days. He existed on

Growers' Disbelief

Many of the grape growers refused to acknowledge that Chavez was engaged in a fast. They simply did not believe he was not eating. They accused one of Chavez's nurses of secretly feeding him. They said she would go out at night and hunt small animals, then cook them and feed them to him when no one was watching.

Chavez laughed at these rumors. He took them as a good sign, because he thought it meant that the growers considered his fast to be a powerful action. If they thought it was meaningless, why would they have cared enough to deny that he was doing it?

very little sleep at that point. Later, he began having pain again. His body weakened, and the lack of nutrients made his bones, muscles, and organs begin to struggle.

THE MEANING

Chavez's fast had more than one meaning. "When any person suffers for someone in greater need, that person is human," he said.[1] Chavez's strong faith taught him that sacrificing to help other people was a good way to live. He had a strong commitment to helping other farmworkers. He was willing to put his life at risk to demonstrate just how much he cared about his fellow Chicanos.

But for him, the fast also had personal, religious significance that many of his colleagues did not understand. Chavez believed that he was getting a spiritual benefit by keeping the discipline of fasting.

Chavez's Words

At the end of his fast, Chavez prepared a statement that was read to the crowd by Reverend James Drake: "The fast has had different meanings for different people. Some of you may still wonder about its meaning and importance. . . . I undertook the fast because my heart was filled with grief and pain for the sufferings of farmworkers. The fast was first for me and then for all of us in this union. It was a fast for nonviolence and a call to sacrifice."[2]

Chavez took communion daily during the fast. A mass was held in his room each day. Within two weeks, Chavez's friends and family began suggesting that the fast had gone on long enough. His doctors were growing very worried about his physical health. Celebrities and politicians sent him notes asking him to please eat. But no one could convince Chavez to stop fasting until he was ready.

A Mass to Break the Fast

On March 10, 1968, approximately 8,000 farmworkers attended a mass to break Chavez's fast. Chavez was now so weak that he could not stand on his own. He had to be carried to the county park, where the service would be conducted. A flatbed truck served as the altar, and there was a large group of priests and nuns present to lead the mass and present communion. Senator Robert F. Kennedy from New York also attended the service. Senator Kennedy presented Chavez with a piece of bread during the service. Chavez broke his fast.

Health and Security

In the year after the fast, Chavez struggled with a painful health issue. He suffered from major back

Chavez was weak from fasting when he sat at a mass with Senator Robert F. Kennedy.

pain. It started with a sharp pain in his back that was so severe that he could not move for 20 minutes. His back troubled him so much that his friends and family became worried. Finally, Chavez saw a special doctor who treated his back. Chavez felt better after the treatment, but his back would continue to be a problem for the rest of his life.

Chavez also received some threats against his life that frightened his family and friends. He was not worried for himself, because he had already proven that he would risk his life to advance the struggle for farmworkers' rights. Chavez said of his added security during that time:

> *There isn't anything that can be done about protection except to make sure that the Union is based not only on myself but on others—and it is. The only way they could protect me is to put me in a bullet-proof tube, or to put me thirty feet underground in a silo. And what work could I do then?[3]*

Still, Chavez allowed guards to accompany him to look out for his safety. He also bought pet German Shepherds for added protection. He named his new security dogs Boycott and Huelga.

Chavez continued his work, trying to negotiate union contracts

Robert F. Kennedy

On March 16, 1968, only six days after the mass to end the fast, Senator Robert F. Kennedy announced that he was running for president. He wanted to follow in the footsteps of his older brother, President John F. Kennedy. President Kennedy had been assassinated in Dallas, Texas, in 1963. He had been a popular leader. The nation was still mourning his death.

Many people believed that electing Senator Robert Kennedy as president would be the next best thing to getting his brother back. Many migrant workers and other Californians, including Chavez, strongly believed this. But some people had not liked President Kennedy and his politics very much. They did not want Senator Kennedy to run for president. One of those people decided not to let him have the chance. Senator Kennedy was assassinated in California on June 6, 1968.

with the California grape growers. As the 1960s
came to a close, the grape boycott and the workers'
strike were still in full force. The union leadership
was struggling to keep them going. But, the grape
growers were also struggling to keep their businesses
afloat. The time to make a deal had finally come. ⌐

Chavez spoke at a news conference in 1968.

On July 29, 1970, grape growers' representatives finally signed a contract with farmworkers.

Si Se Puede:
It Can Be Done

*I*n 1970, Chavez and the grape growers were finally able to sit down to negotiate the terms of a contract for the farmworkers. The contract was signed July 29, 1970. Chavez and other UFW officials met with the growers in Reuther Hall at Forty Acres for the official signing. Many union members were there. They were ready to celebrate. They clapped, cheered, and sang songs of joy as each signature hit the page.

The contracts raised the farmworkers' wage from the previous wage of approximately $1.10 per hour to $1.80 per hour. The growers also agreed to contribute small amounts of money to support the UFW service centers and to the Robert F. Kennedy Health and Welfare Fund. The agreements also contained details on the appropriate use of pesticides.

The signing of these contracts meant that the vast majority (85 percent) of California table grape growers were now under union contracts. This was by far the biggest victory any farmworkers' union had ever accomplished.

The End of La Huelga

Though one piece of the struggle had been resolved, there was still

Sacrifices

As the 29 labor contracts were being signed, Chavez made a few remarks about the difficulties his workers had gone through to maintain the strike for five long years. Since the strike began, the workers had struggled to survive without any pay. Chavez honored the workers' sacrifice with these words: "Ninety five percent of the strikers lost their homes and their cars. But I think that in losing those worldly possessions they found themselves, and they found that only through dedication, through serving mankind, and, in this case, serving the poor, and those who were struggling for justice, only in that way could they really find themselves."[1]

work to be done. Chavez continued his activism and leadership to improve conditions for farmworkers. He negotiated with other unions, trying to find ways for labor contracts to serve both groups' interests well. One group he negotiated with was the Teamsters Union, a truck drivers' union. He also turned his attention to protesting the use of harmful pesticides in grape growing and continued to fight for increased minimum wage for workers.

A New Threat

In the summer of 1971, Chavez received some disturbing news. He was warned of a plot to kill him and burn the records of the UFW. Those who disagreed with the goals that Chavez was working toward had realized that he was not going away. They wanted to do something to stop his movement. Chavez did not want to believe that his life was at risk, but he went into hiding for the month of August. Law enforcement agencies investigated the threat. They learned that a man named Richard Pedigo had been paid $25,000 to kill Chavez. Pedigo was arrested, but it was never determined who had hired him to do the job. He was imprisoned on other charges. The investigation and its unresolved ending led Chavez to believe that someone had indeed been out to kill him. Still, he was unhappy that he had lost a month of work time while hiding.

A Second Fast

On May 11, 1972, Chavez again put his life at risk by fasting. He went to Phoenix, Arizona, for this "fast of love," which was partly meant to protest a new law that had just been passed by the state legislature there. The law would take away the right for farmworkers to boycott or

"To us the boycott of grapes was the most near-perfect of nonviolent struggles, because nonviolence also requires mass involvement. The boycott demonstrated to the whole country, the whole world, what people can do by nonviolent action." [2]

—Cesar Chavez

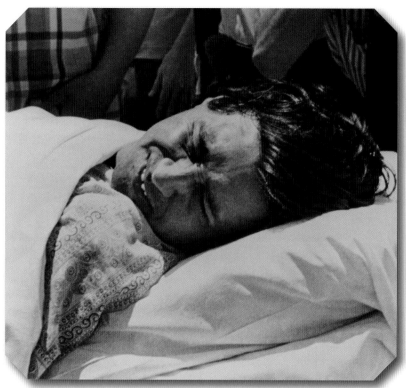

Chavez fasted again in 1972. Fasting was often physically painful for him.

strike. In Arizona, Chavez found that the workers were very discouraged by the new law. They did not believe it was worth fighting anymore, that change was impossible. La Causa adopted a new slogan, *Si Se Puede*, which means, "Yes, it can be done."

Chavez again tried to explain to people that his fasting was not meant as a hunger strike. A hunger strike, he said, would mean he was refusing to eat as a way to put pressure on people to take action. He explained that was not his intention:

> *The fast is a very personal spiritual thing. . . . It's not done out of a desire to destroy myself, but it's done out of a deep conviction that we can communicate to people, either those who are for us or against us, faster and more effectively spiritually than we can in any other way.*[3]

Chavez fasted for 24 days, ending once again with a mass to break his fast.

Slow Progress

La Causa continued to make slow but steady progress. In 1974, the government extended unemployment insurance to cover farmworkers. This meant that during slow economic periods, farmworkers who could not find work would be eligible to apply for unemployment support from the federal government. This was a good victory for farmworkers.

Many of the contracts made with the grape growers in 1970 needed to be renewed in 1973. Chavez had launched a second grape boycott. In 1975, the UFW learned that many Americans were

Proposition 14

After the California Agricultural Labor Relations Act was passed, there were still some debates over certain aspects of the law. The governor appointed a board to oversee the election of officers. One issue they discussed was whether the union organizers could have unlimited access to workers while they were at work on the farms. The UFW wanted access, but the growers wanted the ability to stop union organizers from coming onto their property.

Chavez created Proposition 14, a measure that would allow voters to choose whether or not to support union access. However, some corporate landowners did not want the proposition to pass. They pooled their money and made advertisements that discouraged voters from supporting Chavez. Their efforts worked — Proposition 14 was voted down on Election Day.

participating in this boycott. In fact, a poll revealed that 17 million Americans had joined the grape boycott. The UFW was gaining impressive support.

Agricultural Labor Relations Act

In 1975, La Causa had another big success. The Agricultural Labor Relations Act was passed in California. It was the first law concerning farm labor organizing that had ever been signed in the continental United States.

This was a huge victory for Chavez and the UFW. The Agricultural Labor Relations Act officially gave unions legal power to organize workers. The law secured their right to boycott and vote for officers. It also gave migrant workers the right to participate in elections. This helped ensure that the farmworkers would be treated fairly in the future.

PESTICIDES

Over the next ten years, Chavez began adding a new focus to his work. The UFW began formally protesting the use of pesticides in agriculture, especially in grape growing. In the late 1960s, a number of migrant workers had grown ill and been hospitalized with symptoms of pesticide poisoning. Illnesses continued among workers in the 1970s and 1980s, because the growers would not stop the use of pesticides.

Chavez began to speak to environmentalists about the dangerous chemicals being

Pesticides

In farming, pesticides are substances used to control insects and other small organisms that may feed on or harm plants. Use of pesticides in the United States is regulated by the Environmental Protection Agency. Different pesticides receive safety ratings on a toxicity scale, from nontoxic to extremely toxic. Pesticides that receive high toxicity ratings may be outlawed or restricted from sale to the general public. Farmers can take a test and pay to gain a license to use dangerous pesticides that are banned from the public.

Toxic pesticides can damage humans in many ways. Long-term exposure to some pesticides may make it more likely for people to get cancer and other serious illnesses. Babies born to women who have pesticide poisoning are more likely to have serious birth defects. Pesticides also seep through the ground and may contaminate the drinking water in an entire region. As people grow more concerned about the environmental and health effects of pesticides, researchers have worked to develop safer pesticides for use on farms. They may try to create pesticides out of natural ingredients, using fewer or mild chemicals.

used in farming, especially in grape vineyards. He initiated another boycott of grapes, and many consumers who supported better environmental practices for farming joined in the protest.

In 1987, the UFW produced a film called *The Wrath of Grapes,* which explained the dangers of pesticide use. The film exposed the risks workers face by constantly touching and breathing in the fumes of pesticides. These workers could end up facing cancer, lung problems, and birth defects in their children. The film's title was a play on the name of a famous novel about migrant workers, *The Grapes of Wrath,* by John Steinbeck.

In 1988 Chavez was 61 years old, and he engaged in his third public fast. The purpose this time was to protest the use of pesticides and to gain more attention for the ongoing grape boycott. This fast was his longest, lasting 36 days. ⌐

In 1985, Chavez protested the use of pesticides on grapes.

Chavez continued his work with the UFW into the 1990s.

LATER LIFE AND LEGACY

esar Chavez expected to live a long and healthy life, as long as he could manage to avoid accidents or violence at the hands of his opponents. Family history contributed to this belief. Chavez's grandmother had lived to be almost

100 years old. His mother had lived to be 99, and his father had not died until reaching age 101. Chavez himself would not be so fortunate.

Chavez was in the middle of a difficult court trial in Yuma, Arizona, in April 1993. He had been sitting in court, testifying, for two days. He was under great stress. The UFW was being sued for millions of dollars by corporate landowners. Winning this court case was very important to the organization's financial future. On the evening of April 23, 1993, Chavez returned to the house where he was staying. He was very tired and distraught over the seriousness of the trial. He met briefly with UFW officers, prepared and ate his dinner, then retired to his room.

Chavez died in his sleep that night at just 66 years old. He had been an activist to the end. In the morning, his friends came to wake him and found that he had passed away. He was still wearing his clothes, and he had a book about Native American artifacts in his hand.

Cesar Chavez's sudden death was a huge shock to those who knew and admired him. It was so unexpected that some of Chavez's followers briefly suspected that he had been murdered by his enemies.

But those who were with him that night felt sure there had been no foul play. His autopsy confirmed that he had died in his sleep. Family members later indicated that the cause of death was a pulmonary embolism, a blood clot that damaged his lungs. He was also likely still in a weakened state overall, as he was recovering from a recent eight-day spiritual fast.

FAREWELL TO A LEADER

Less than a week later, nearly 40,000 people attended the funeral mass for Chavez. The ceremony was held on April 29 in Delano. People traveled from all over California and the rest of the nation to pay their respects. The massive crowd gathered in Memorial Park, and they completed a three-mile (4.8-km) funeral march to Forty Acres. When the front of the crowd reached their destination, the back of the line had

Standing in Solidarity

Chavez never forgot where he came from, even though he became a national hero. Chavez led a simple life, similar to that of the migrant workers he represented. He never purchased a house or a car of his own. He never earned more than $6,000 per year. By the time of his death in 1993, a full-time minimum wage worker in the United States was earning approximately $8,500 per year.

Chavez once said, "It's ironic that those who till the soil, cultivate and harvest the fruits, vegetables and other foods that fill your tables with abundance, have nothing left for themselves."[1]

*Many people participated in a three-mile (4.8-km)
funeral procession for Chavez.*

not yet left Memorial Park. The line of mourners
stretched long enough to fill the full three miles.

The coffin at the head of the procession was a
plain pine box, built by Chavez's brother Richard.
Chavez's son Paul commented that the unadorned
box was exactly what his father would have preferred.
True to Chavez's life of poverty and sacrifice, his
family wished to demonstrate that a fancy coffin was
not needed to show that the person inside had been
well loved.

Cardinal Roger Mahoney, a longtime supporter of Cesar Chavez and the union, led the funeral mass. Numerous speakers offered eulogies, and letters were read from the president of the United States, the president of Mexico, and the pope, among other famous politicians and leaders. The following day, Chavez was buried in La Paz, near the new headquarters of the UFW.

POSTHUMOUS HONORS

One year after Chavez died, a commemorative march from Delano to Sacramento honored his historic pilgrimage of 1966. The march was led by Chavez's successor, Arturo Rodriguez, the new leader of the UFW. Later that year, on August 8, 1994, President Bill Clinton honored Cesar Chavez with the Medal of Freedom, which is the nation's highest civilian honor. The award was given posthumously, which

A Simple Eulogy

When Cesar Chavez died, important people throughout the world sent their condolences. However, in his humility and simplicity, Chavez probably would have liked best the comments he received from his fellow farmworkers. Even after he became famous, he considered himself to be the same, no better or worse, than the farmworkers he once labored beside. One fieldworker, Manuel Amaya, said, "God has taken the strongest arm that we have, but we will continue."[2]

means after death. Helen Chavez attended a ceremony at the White House and accepted the medal on behalf of her husband.

In 2000, California declared Chavez's birthday, March 31, a state holiday. The holiday is called Cesar E. Chavez Day. It is a day for people to remember the importance of providing service to their communities and to honor Chavez's work. As of 2010, nine other states recognized the day with commemorative events.

In 2006, Cesar Chavez was one of 11 individuals inducted into the California Hall of Fame. It was the first year for the Hall of Fame. Chavez's supporters knew that he was an ideal person to be included in this list.

On September 4, 2008, hundreds of people gathered at San Jose State University in San Jose,

Postage Stamp

On September 18, 2002, the U.S. Postal Service announced its plan to honor Cesar Chavez by putting his image on a first-class postage stamp. The stamp image featured a close-up painting of Chavez's smiling face. In the background was a green field planted with rows of crops. His name appeared in capital letters at the bottom.

Benjamin Ocasio, vice president of diversity for the U.S. Postal Service, spoke at the unveiling ceremony. "The significance of his impact transcends any one cause or struggle," Ocasio said. "This leader is a welcome and important addition to the nation's stamp program."[3]

The 37-cent Cesar E. Chavez stamp was released in April 2003.

California, for the dedication of the Cesar E. Chavez Monument. The monument is called the Arch of Dignity, Equality and Justice. The monument will stand in honor of La Causa and Cesar Chavez's contributions for years to come.

A Library of Resources

Jacques E. Levy, a journalist who wrote a comprehensive biography of Cesar Chavez and La Causa, wanted to do something to help preserve Chavez's legacy. Levy had spent about six years shadowing Chavez through his daily routine. Levy interviewed Chavez

Cesar E. Chavez Day

Cesar E. Chavez Day is an important day for many people in the United States. Part of this day is celebrating the achievements that Chavez made. In Los Angeles, California, people attend the Cesar E. Chavez Day parade. They might even see famous actors and musicians participating in the celebration.

Many people spend the day doing service activities to contribute to their communities, just as Chavez worked to help his community of farmworkers. People might plant gardens in their communities, donate to food shelves, or work to improve the natural environment. Some people in California celebrate by gathering a group of volunteers and building playgrounds in California communities. In 2008, they built ten playgrounds.

By 2010, Arizona, California, Colorado, Illinois, Michigan, New Mexico, Rhode Island, Texas, Utah, and Wisconsin all recognized Cesar E. Chavez Day. However, California was the only state to make it a legal state holiday. Many people were working with petitions to help make Cesar E. Chavez Day a national holiday. They felt that everyone should learn about Chavez and be reminded of the importance of helping one's community.

as well as a number of his colleagues, making notes for the book. After Chavez died, Levy put together a collection of the taped interviews, notes, and media clippings from the research he had done in writing his book. Levy also interviewed Chavez's family and close friends shortly after his death and added those tapes to the collection. He turned all of the materials over to the Yale University Library, where students and researchers could access the information. Levy hoped that his own work studying La Causa and its leader would be useful to future scholars who might choose to study the roots of the migrant worker organizing movement.

Many of Chavez's own papers are kept at the Farm Workers Archive, located in a library at Wayne State University in Detroit, Michigan. More papers can be found in the San Joaquin Valley Farm Workers' collection at Fresno State University Library in Fresno, California. Many people are committed to preserving Chavez's legacy by maintaining these resources.

LEGACY

In 1968, Senator Robert F. Kennedy referred to Cesar Chavez as "one of the heroic figures of our time."[4] Cesar Chavez certainly lived up to this label. His legacy continues in the ongoing work of the migrant workers' union he initiated. The continued work of his followers will ensure that future generations of migrant workers remember Chavez's name, and that all Americans remain aware of his contributions to their nation's history.

"The end of all knowledge should be service to others," Chavez said.[5] Enacting this philosophy, he lived his life with humility. It is why he personally made sacrifice after sacrifice for the betterment of humanity. It is why the world will always remember Cesar Chavez and his vision for La Causa.

Migrant Workers Today

Cesar Chavez's movement brought awareness of migrant labor conditions to the public. His work also united Mexican Americans to fight for change. But that change has been slow to come. The work and living conditions of migrant workers has not improved much over time. Today it is estimated that there are between 2 and 3 million migrant workers in the workforce. Many of them still face issues such as low pay.

The Cesar E. Chavez Monument was created to honor the people involved in La Causa.

TIMELINE

1927	1937	1944
Cesar Chavez is born near Yuma, Arizona, on March 31.	On August 29, the Chavez family farm is repossessed.	Chavez enlists in the U.S. Navy at age 17.

1965	1965	1966
On September 16, the NFWA joins a strike against California grape growers.	The NFWA begins the first grape boycotts in November and December.	The march to Sacramento begins in Delano, California, on March 17.

1948

Chavez marries Helen Favela on October 22.

1962

On March 31, Chavez resigns from his position as national director of the Community Service Organization.

1962

The first meeting of the National Farm Workers Association is held in Fresno, California, on September 30.

1966

On April 10, more than 10,000 participants in the march to Sacramento arrive at the capitol building.

1968

On February 16, Chavez begins a fast to inspire his followers to commit to nonviolence.

1968

Senator Robert F. Kennedy and 8,000 farmworkers attend a mass to break Chavez's fast on March 10.

TIMELINE

1970

On July 29, grape growers sign contracts with the UFW, ending the strike and the grape boycott.

1972

On May 11, Chavez again puts his life at risk by fasting, this time for 24 days.

1973

Chavez launches a second grape boycott.

1993

Chavez dies in his sleep on April 23.

1993

A procession follows Chavez's coffin to his funeral mass at Forty Acres on April 29.

1994

Chavez's successor, Arturo Rodriguez, leads a commemorative march from Delano to Sacramento in April.

1975

The Agricultural Labor Relations Act is passed in California.

1987

The UFW produces *The Wrath of Grapes,* a film about the dangers of pesticide use in farming.

1988

Chavez fasts for 36 days to protest pesticide use.

1994

President Bill Clinton posthumously honors Chavez with the Medal of Freedom on August 8.

2006

Chavez is inducted into the California Hall of Fame on December 6.

2008

The Cesar E. Chavez monument is dedicated on September 4.

Essential Facts

Date of Birth

March 31, 1927

Place of Birth

near Yuma, Arizona

Date of Death

April 23, 1993

Parents

Juana and Librado Chavez

Education

Chavez attended more than 30 schools in his lifetime. He dropped out of school after eighth grade to become a farmworker.

Marriage

Helen Favela (October 22, 1948)

Children

Fernando, Sylvia, Linda, Eloise, Anna, Paul, Elizabeth, and Anthony

Career Highlights

In 1966, Chavez led a crowd of more than 10,000 people for 340 miles (550 km) in the march to Sacramento. He also helped pass the Agricultural Labor Relations Act in 1975. This act gave unions legal power to organize workers.

Societal Contribution

Chavez worked to give Chicanos a voice in politics by registering new voters. He helped obtain fair pay, hours, and working conditions for farmworkers in the United States. He warned communities about the dangers of using pesticides on crops.

Conflicts

Chavez fought against farm owners to obtain better pay and working conditions for farmworkers. The FBI investigated Chavez as a communist when he was working with the Community Service Organization. In 1971, Chavez learned his life was in danger and went into hiding for a month.

Quote

"The greatest tragedy is not to live and die, as we all must. The greatest tragedy is for a person to live and die without knowing the satisfaction of giving life for others."—*Cesar Chavez*

ADDITIONAL RESOURCES

SELECT BIBLIOGRAPHY

Del Castillo, Richard Griswold, and Richard A. Garcia. *César Chávez: A Triumph of Spirit*. Norman, OK: University of Oklahoma Press, 1995.

Levy, Jacques E. *Cesar Chavez: Autobiography of La Causa*. Minneapolis, MN: University of Minnesota Press, 2007.

Menchaca, Martha. *The Mexican Outsiders*. Austin, TX: University of Texas Press, 1995.

FURTHER READING

Alegre, Cesar. *Extraordinary Hispanic Americans*. New York, NY: Scholastic, 2007.

Chavez, Cesar. *An Organizer's Tale: Speeches*. New York, NY: Penguin, 2008.

Delano, Marfé Ferguson. *American Heroes*. Washington, DC: National Geographic, 2005.

WEB LINKS

To learn more about Cesar Chavez, visit ABDO Publishing Company online at **www.abdopublishing.com**. Web sites about Cesar Chavez are featured on our Book Links page. These links are routinely monitored and updated to provide the most current information available.

Places to Visit

The California Museum
1020 O Street, Sacramento, CA 92814
916-653-7524
www.californiamuseum.org
The museum houses the California Hall of Fame, into which Cesar
Chavez was inducted in 2006.

Cesar E. Chavez Community Action Center
San Jose State University, Building BB, #105
One Washington Square, San Jose, CA 95192-0265
408-924-4144
www.as.sjsu.edu/cccac
This organization works to promote and provide community
service opportunities.

The National Chavez Center
29700 Woodford-Tehachapi Road, Keene, CA 93531
661-823-6134
www.nationalchavezcenter.org
This educational facility includes a visitor center, a museum,
and a conference center. It also houses Chavez's papers.

GLOSSARY

agriculture
> Farming.

boycott
> A form of protest in which citizens refuse to buy certain goods or engage in certain activities.

bracero
> An immigrant worker hired to replace a local migrant worker at a lower wage.

capitalism
> An economic system in which the means of production are privately owned and which is governed by the principles of a free market economy: supply and demand.

Chicano
> A person of Mexican descent.

civil disobedience
> Actions such as trespassing and minor vandalism, illegal but usually nonviolent, in which activists hope to make political statements.

communion
> A holy feast of bread and wine for Christians.

communism
> An ideology pursuing a classless society based on the common ownership of the means of production.

demonstration
> A public protest against an unfair law or activity.

growers
> Farm owners.

Hispanic
> Of Spanish origin or descent.

immigrant
> A person who moves to one country from another country.

integrate
> To combine groups regardless of race, class, gender, or ethnic group.

La Causa
> The cause; the name of the organizing movement Chavez led.

La Huelga
> The strike.

labor union
> A group of workers who unite to protect their jobs and improve their work conditions.

mass
> A worship service in the Roman Catholic religious tradition.

migrant worker
> A person who travels from state to state for work, usually to work on farms.

minimum wage
> The lowest amount a worker can legally be paid for one hour of work.

mission
> A church or station where people perform religious work.

nonviolence
> A philosophy of peaceful resistance.

pesticide
> A chemical used to kill insects that harm plants.

strike
> A temporary stoppage of work by employees who demand higher pay or improved conditions.

vineyard
> A farm where grapes are grown.

Source Notes

Chapter 1. 340 Miles
1. Cesar Chavez. *An Organizer's Tale: Speeches.* New York, NY: Penguin, 2008. xx.

Chapter 2. Childhood
1. Jacques E. Levy. *Cesar Chavez: Autobiography of La Causa.* Minneapolis, MN: University of Minnesota Press, 2007. 23.
2. Richard Griswold del Castillo and Richard A. Garcia. *César Chávez: A Triumph of Spirit.* Norman, OK: University of Oklahoma Press, 1995. 13.
3. Cesar Chavez. "History." *United Farm Workers.* 25 Sept. 2008 <http://www.ufw.org/_page.php?menu=research&inc=history/09.html>.

Chapter 3. Young Adulthood
1. Cesar Chavez. *An Organizer's Tale: Speeches.* New York, NY: Penguin, 2008. 235–236.
2. Jacques E. Levy. *Cesar Chavez: Autobiography of La Causa.* Minneapolis, MN: University of Minnesota Press, 2007. 102.

Chapter 4. Emerging Leader

1. Richard Griswold del Castillo and Richard A. Garcia. *César Chávez: A Triumph of Spirit.* Norman, OK: University of Oklahoma Press, 1995. 25.

Chapter 5. Back to Delano

1. Richard Griswold del Castillo and Richard A. Garcia. *César Chávez: A Triumph of Spirit.* Norman, OK: University of Oklahoma Press, 1995. 33.
2. Jacques E. Levy. *Cesar Chavez: Autobiography of La Causa.* Minneapolis, MN: University of Minnesota Press, 2007. 467.
3. Cesar Chavez. *An Organizer's Tale: Speeches.* New York, NY: Penguin, 2008. xvii.

Source Notes Continued

Chapter 6. March to Sacramento
1. Cesar Chavez. *An Organizer's Tale: Speeches.* New York, NY: Penguin, 2008. xvii–xviii.
2. Cesar Chavez. "Cesar Chavez: Farm, Union Is Alive, Well." *Los Angeles Times.* 2 Jan. 1975: 7(II).
3. Jacques E. Levy. *Cesar Chavez: Autobiography of La Causa.* Minneapolis, MN: University of Minnesota Press, 2007. 272.

Chapter 7. Fasting, Strikes, and Boycotts
1. Cesar Chavez. *An Organizer's Tale: Speeches.* New York, NY: Penguin, 2008. xxii–xxiii.
2. Ibid. 47–48.
3. Jacques E. Levy. *Cesar Chavez: Autobiography of La Causa.* Minneapolis, MN: University of Minnesota Press, 2007. 262.

Chapter 8. Si Se Puede: It Can Be Done
1. Richard Griswold del Castillo and Richard A. Garcia. *César Chávez: A Triumph of Spirit.* Norman, OK: University of Oklahoma Press, 1995. 94.
2. Jacques E. Levy. *Cesar Chavez: Autobiography of La Causa.* Minneapolis, MN: University of Minnesota Press, 2007. 269.
3. Ibid. 465.

Chapter 9. Later Life and Legacy

1. Cesar Chavez. *An Organizer's Tale: Speeches.* New York, NY: Penguin, 2008. 236.

2. Richard Griswold del Castillo and Richard A. Garcia. *César Chávez: A Triumph of Spirit.* Norman, OK: University of Oklahoma Press, 1995. 174.

3. United States Postal Service. "Cesar E. Chavez Postage Stamp Unveiled at United States Capitol." *Philatelic News.* 18 Sept. 2002. <http://www.usps.com/news/2002/philatelic/sr02_072.htm>.

4. Cesar Chavez. *An Organizer's Tale: Speeches.* New York, NY: Penguin, 2008. back cover.

5. Ibid. vii.

INDEX

ABOUT THE AUTHOR

Kekla Magoon is the author of fiction and nonfiction books for young adults. She especially enjoys writing about history and social studies. Her young adult novel *The Rock and the River* was published in January 2009.

PHOTO CREDITS

Arthur Schatz/Time Life Pictures/Getty Images, cover, 46, 65; Sal Veder/AP Images, 6; AP Images, 9, 15, 27, 37, 45, 60, 66, 75, 80, 85, 98 (top), 99; Walter R. Reuther Library/Wayne State University, 16; tm/© 2009 the Cesar E. Chavez Foundation www.chavezfoundation.org and Walter R. Reuther Library/Wayne State University, 24, 41; Library of Congress, 28, 96 (top); Gary Kazanjian/AP Images, 32; Hulton Archive/Getty Images, 38; George Birc/AP Images, 52; Barry Sweet/AP Images, 55, 96 (bottom); Ted Streshinsky/Corbis, 56; Michael Rougler/Time Life Pictures/Getty Images, 72, 97; Bettmann/Corbis, 76; Alan Greth/AP Images, 86; Bob Galbraith/AP Images, 89, 98 (bottom); Paul Sakuma/AP Images, 95